YOU'VE BEEN GRANTED: A JOURNEY OF FAITH, RESPONSIBILITY AND BECOMING

DR. BURGUNDY ROYSTER

YOU'VE BEEN GRANTED: A JOURNEY OF FAITH, RESPONSIBILITY AND BECOMING

Copyright © 2025
All rights reserved.

Published by **Twenty Pearls Publishing Co.**

No part of this book may be reproduced, distributed, transmitted, or stored in any form or by any means—electronic, mechanical, photocopying, recording, or otherwise—without the prior written permission of the publisher, except in the case of brief quotations used in reviews or scholarly works.

This book is a work of nonfiction. Certain names, personal details, and events may have been changed to protect the privacy of individuals. Any resemblance to actual persons, living or deceased, or actual events is coincidental unless otherwise stated.

The information contained in this book is provided for educational and inspirational purposes only. It does not constitute legal, tax, financial, or professional advice. Readers should consult appropriate professionals regarding their individual circumstances. Neither the publisher nor the author assumes any liability for actions taken based on the contents of this book.

ISBN: 979-8-9932163-1-7

Printed in the United States of America
First Edition

DEDICATION PAGE

To my mother, Kian Milton,

For every late night, every sacrifice, every moment you chose to give when you had nothing left to give—thank you.

You taught me to be strong, to lead with faith, and to rise above my circumstances. You believed in me before I believed in myself.

This book, every page of it, is proof of your love and strength.

It isn't just my story.
It's yours.

CONTENTS

DEDICATION PAGE iii
FOREWORD v
ACKNOWLEDGEMENTS viii
HUMBLE BEGINNINGS IN CORSICANA 12
LIFE AS THE OLDEST SIBLING 19
LESSONS FROM LOSS AND LOVE 32
COLLEGE, CAREER DREAMS & LOVE 47
FROM TURBO TAX TO TAX PRO 61
THE BIRTH OF GRANTED TAX SERVICE 75
CLIMBING THE BUSINESS LADDER 88
CREATING "THE GRANT" METHODOLOGY . 100
NATIONAL RECOGNITION & FEATURES 114
BECOMING A COACH, A CEO AND AN AUTHOR 127
BORN FOR A PURPOSE 141
BROKEN BUT STILL STANDING 152
THE DAY EVERYTHING CHANGED 169
CHRISTMAS LOST ITS MAGIC 184
ABOUT THE AUTHOR 198

FOREWORD

As a tax attorney that represent tax professionals, I have witnessed the weight that our nation's tax system places on individuals, families, and small business owners. I have also witnessed how the right guidance — rooted in integrity and expertise — can transform confusion into clarity and despair into empowerment. Dr. Burgundy Royster Grant embodies that transformation.

Burgundy is not simply a tax professional; she is a strategist, an educator, and a trailblazer. Where many see tax preparation as a seasonal task, she sees it as a lifelong tool for building legacy. She has taken a profession often reduced to forms and deadlines and elevated it into a mission of service and empowerment.

Her journey is one that commands respect. From growing up in an environment where expectations were limited, she carved out her own path. She was not armed with privilege, but with grit, faith, and an unshakable commitment to excellence. The result is more than a thriving business. It is a movement that is rooted in education, accountability, and transformation.

In the legal field, we often speak of precedent, which are the cases that shape the future. In her industry,

Burgundy has become that precedent. Through Granted Tax Service, the Grant Methodology, and her unwavering advocacy for financial literacy, she has set a new standard for what it means to be a tax professional.

This book is both a testimony and teaching tool. It offers readers an inside look at how determination can overcome disadvantage, how vision can overcome limitation, and how one professional's calling can elevate an entire community. It is as much about personal perseverance as it is about professional mastery.

As you read these pages, you will find yourself inspired not only by Dr. Burgundy Royster Grant's story, but also by her systems, strategies, and principles. Whether you are a tax preparer, a small business owner, or simply someone seeking to reclaim control over your financial story, this book will remind you that success leaves a blueprint and Burgundy has laid it out here with honesty and heart.

It is my privilege, as a fellow guardian of justice in the tax field, to introduce you to this extraordinary work. May it challenge you, guide you, and most importantly, remind you that your story, like Burgundy's is still being written.

ACKNOWLEDGEMENTS

I would first like to thank God, whose grace, favor, and guidance have carried me through every challenge and triumph. Without Him, none of this would exist. Every lesson, every blessing, every opportunity is a reflection of His plan for my life.

To my husband, Byron Grant—thank you for being my partner in every season, for your encouragement, patience, and belief in me when I questioned myself. You've been my sounding board, my anchor, and my biggest supporter.

To my siblings—Isis, Winter, and Tre—thank you for giving me another reason to keep pushing. You've reminded me why generational change matters, and every milestone I achieve is also for you.

To my Granted Tax Service team—you are the heartbeat of this business. Thank you for believing in my vision, for showing up for our clients, and for committing to excellence. Together, we are not just preparing taxes—we're preparing legacies.

To my mentees and coaching clients—thank you for trusting me to guide you. Your successes inspire me daily, and watching you grow your businesses and futures has been one of the most rewarding parts of my journey.

Finally, to every client, reader, and supporter — thank you for allowing me to serve you. Your trust fuels my purpose, and your success stories keep me going, even in the toughest seasons.

This book is for all of you — those who believed, supported, and stood by me as I turned my struggles into strength and my purpose into a platform.

x

ONE

HUMBLE BEGINNINGS in CORSICANA

Corsicana, Texas, may have been where Dr. Burgundy Royster entered the world, but her story would soon shift to places far more defining. Born on December 9, 1991, Burgundy came into the world as the first and only child of Kian Milton, a resilient single mother with a fire in her heart and determination in her spirit. My mom was the type of woman who did what had to be done, even when resources were scarce, and time was tight.

At just five years old, Burgundy and her mother relocated from Corsicana to a rough neighborhood known as Highland Hills. Highland Hills was a world of its own a place marked by struggle, survival, and a deep-rooted sense of community. The streets were tough, and the environment could break you if you let it. But it was here that Burgundy's sense of purpose and ambition started to take root.

My mom worked multiple jobs to provide for her daughter, making sure I never felt the weight of their circumstances more than the strength of her love. Our home wasn't fancy, but it was full of warmth, laughter, and a clear message: "This might be where we are now, but it won't be where we finish."

Growing up in Highland Hills taught me how to read people, how to move wisely, and how to protect my peace. She saw things children shouldn't have to see. She heard gunshots some nights instead of lullabies. She knew what it meant to struggle, but more importantly, she learned what it meant to survive.

Despite the challenges, I was a bright and

curious child. I was sharp beyond my years, always asking questions, always seeking more. I played volleyball and ran track, using sports as an outlet and a path to something better. My mother made sure that I was enrolled in schools within the Dallas Independent School District, and the education I had received there opened up a new world of possibilities.

I graduated from A. Maceo Smith High School, where I continued to thrive academically and athletically. Every obstacle in Highland Hills only fueled her determination to rise above it. She had goals bigger than her ZIP code. Even then, she knew she wasn't meant to be average.

Later, she attended the University of North Texas and Navarro College, eventually earning her Ph.D. in Lafayette, Louisiana. But long before any degree or diploma, I had already passed the hardest test of all—growing up in an environment that didn't expect much from me and choosing to rise anyway.

She still remembers a conversation in her teens when someone joked about her doing taxes, maybe with TurboTax. At the time, she laughed it off. But that moment stayed with her. The seed was planted, even if she didn't realize it right away.

Looking back, Highland Hills didn't hold me back, it shaped me. It sharpened my instincts, deepened my faith, and gave her a testimony. My story was just the beginning, and it started not with privilege or promise, but with pressure, pain, and the unshakable belief that there had to be more.

And there was.

TWO

LIFE AS The OLDEST SIBLING

Being an only child for many years gave me a certain kind of independence. It was just me and my mother, navigating life together. For a long time, it felt like the two of us were all we had. But that dynamic shifted in a beautiful and challenging way when myself became a big sister — and not just any big sister, but the kind whose siblings would look at me as part sister, part second mom, and full-time protector.

Years after I had already started charting my path in life, my mother gave birth to three more children: Isis, Tre, and Winter. The age gaps between us were significant—Isis came 16 years after me, Tre followed 18 years after, and winter, the youngest, was born 21 years after me. I was no longer just a daughter—I was now the oldest sibling with a heavy title and even heavier responsibility.

Most people become older siblings with a few years' head start. I, on the other hand, was a teenager when my siblings were born and a young adult when they entered early childhood. I wasn't just around for their toddler years—I helped shape them. I wasn't watching cartoons with them, I was watching their development, watching over their safety, watching out for things they were too young to understand.

From the moment Isis was born, something in me shifted. I had felt a deep, instant need to show up—not just as a big sister, but as a role model. I understood from my own life that children absorb their environment. They listen to what's said and what's not said. They watch what you do more than what you tell them.

And so, I made it my mission to show my siblings what it meant to overcome.

At times, it felt like I was living two lives. While most young women my age were out discovering themselves, I was juggling work, school, and sibling duty. I'd rock my sister to sleep and then go pull an all-nighter for an exam. I'd buy groceries with my own money to make sure the house had what it needed. I didn't complain. I didn't brag. I just did it. Because in her heart, it was never a burden — it was love.

I remember moments like helping Isis with her

homework, teaching Winter how to tie her shoes, and keeping Tre occupied while our mother worked. I wasn't their parent—but in many moments, I had to be. And that created a bond deeper than most siblings ever get the chance to build.

But being the oldest wasn't just about nurturing, it was also about protecting. Highland Hills wasn't the safest place to raise children, and I knew what would happen if you didn't watch closely. I made it my job to keep my siblings aware but not afraid, smart but not hardened. I taught them how to carry themselves with pride, how to stay out of trouble, how to move carefully in a world that didn't always play fair.

They looked up to me. And not because I asked them to, but because I gave them something to believe in. They saw me going to school, handling business, staying focused, and refusing to settle. They heard other people talk about how "Burgundy got it together." They knew that when they were in doubt, they could call me. And that's exactly what they did.

There's a certain pressure that comes with

being the blueprint. When you're the first, everything you do is either an example or a warning. I took that responsibility seriously. I understood that my decisions would ripple through the lives of my younger siblings. If I succeed, it will give them permission to believe they could too. If I failed, I also knew the consequences would hit more than just me.

That kind of weight makes you grow up faster. But it also gives you a deep sense of purpose. For me, my siblings became a constant reminder of why I had to keep going—even when it was hard. Even when I was tired. Even when I felt like giving up.

As the years passed, my life began to flourish. I was building my business, getting my education, and earning respect. But through it all, I never disconnected from my siblings. I stayed involved. I showed up to birthdays, and hard conversations. I poured into them — mentally, emotionally, and spiritually.

Each sibling brought something different into my life.
Isis, the oldest of the three, was fiery, intelligent, and full of curiosity. She reminded

me of myself in so many ways, quick-witted, observant, and unafraid to question the world around her.

Tre, the middle child, was sensitive, creative, and expressive. He is also autistic. He brought a softness that made me pause and appreciate the beauty in stillness.

Winter, the baby of the family, was full of energy, laughter, and potential. Watching her grow gave me a renewed sense of urgency to secure the family's future.

I wasn't just mentoring them — I was shaping the family legacy. And that legacy wasn't rooted in perfection, but in progress. It was built on real-life lessons, spiritual faith, and an unbreakable bond that went beyond bloodlines.

I often say that being the oldest sibling taught me more about leadership than any classroom ever could. It taught me how to listen without judgment. How to discipline with love. How to balance accountability with grace. It gave me the patience to train others later in life — whether it was my tax team, my clients, or my coaching students.

I have also learned how to carry myself with strength in front of others, even when I was struggling behind the scenes. Because when you're the oldest, people don't always check on you—they assume you've got it all together. But I knew how to find my release. I'd pray. I'd write. I'd reflect. And then I'd rise and do it all again.

Even now, as a CEO, a tax coach, and soon-to-be author, I still carry my role as the oldest sister with pride. I'll never forget where I started, or who was watching me along the way.

Being the oldest wasn't a job I had asked for, it was one I embraced. It shaped my identity, my leadership style, and my mission. I wasn't just trying to succeed for myself. I was breaking generational barriers so my siblings could walk through doors she had to fight to open.

And as they grew, they began to understand just how much their big sister had done for them—not just in words, but in action.
Because I wasn't just the oldest sibling.
I was the example.

THREE

LESSONS from LOSS and LOVE

Life doesn't always wait for you to be ready. Sometimes, it just throws you into the fire and watches to see what you'll do with the heat. I didn't ask for the lesson's life gave me — especially the ones wrapped in heartbreak and silence — but I see now that they were shaping me into the woman I was always meant to be. Growing up, love was all around me, though not always in the form I expected. My mother was the first to show me what love looked like. She was the kind of woman who sacrificed without needing applause, who made sure we had what we needed even when she went without. She taught me love through action. She taught me that real love shows up, even when it's tiring, even when it hurts.

I saw love in my siblings too. We laughed together, fought like cats and dogs, but always came back to each other. That bond was unspoken but unbreakable. It was a kind of safety net that let me know no matter what life threw at me, I wasn't alone. That kind of love taught me about loyalty, about forgiveness, and about showing up even when it's not convenient.

But then came the kind of love that makes your heart race. The kind you dream about. The kind that sweeps in and makes you feel like maybe, just maybe, life is finally giving you something sweet. My early relationships were filled with hope and dreams, with visions of forever. But they also came with betrayal, abandonment, and disappointment.

I learned quickly that not everyone who says they love you knows how to love you right. Some people love you based on their capacity, not your worth. And when they fall short, it can leave you questioning everything — your value, your beauty, your enoughness.

I remember lying in bed one night after yet another heartbreak, staring at the ceiling, trying to figure out what was wrong with me. I replayed every conversation, every moment, looking for a clue that would explain why I wasn't enough to be chosen, to be cherished. That kind of pain isn't just emotional, it's physical. It tightens your chest, weighs on your spirit, and makes you question if you'll ever truly be seen.

But nothing could've prepared me for the kind of loss that came next.

There is no heartbreak like losing a child. Especially one you've never held but already loved with every fiber of your being. When I first found out I was pregnant, it felt like everything in my world aligned. It was joy. It was purpose. It was possibility. I imagined tiny fingers wrapping around mine, soft cries in the night, first steps, birthday candles. I dreamed of the whole future in just a few weeks.

And then—just like that—it was gone. The silence of that ultrasound room is something I'll never forget. The absence of a heartbeat echoed louder than any scream. I remember holding my breath, hoping the silence was a mistake. Maybe the machine was wrong. That maybe I had just misunderstood.

But no. The life I had carried inside of me was gone before I ever got to meet them.

That grief is a silent companion. It doesn't announce itself loudly like other pain. It shows up in quiet moments. It lingers in the background while life goes on around you. It watches you smile and laugh and carry on, all while reminding you that something precious is missing.

I grieved deeply. Not just once. Not just for one child. But for multiple losses. Each one leaving a scar that the world couldn't see but that I could feel every day. And what made it even harder was the world's silence around that kind of pain. People don't always know what to say, so they say nothing. But that silence? It can feel like isolation. Like your grief doesn't matter. Like your babies didn't matter.

I started questioning everything — my body, my purpose, my faith, even my womanhood. Was I broken? Was I being punished? Was I not worthy of the blessing so many others seemed to receive with ease?

I watched others celebrate their pregnancies, their gender reveals, their baby showers, and I smiled, because I was genuinely happy for them. But I also ached. I wondered, "Why not me?" And that question haunted me through nights filled with tears and prayers.

There were days I wanted to give up. Days when the pain was so heavy that breathing felt like a task. I went through the motions—work, family, social events—masking my heartbreak with makeup and small talk. But inside, I was drowning.

Still, through all of it, there was a whisper. A quiet voice that said, "You're still here. You still have work to do."

That whisper saved me. It didn't shout. It didn't drag me out of my sorrow. It just reminded me that there was more to my story. That these losses weren't the end of me.

Slowly, I began to rise.

It wasn't immediate. Healing never is. It's messy. It's nonlinear. Some days you feel strong, and others you're back on the floor, crying over memories and moments that will never be. But I kept going. One breath at a time. One prayer at a time. One act of self-love at a time.

I started to redefine love.

Love, I realized, isn't just about romance. It's not about someone choosing you or staying. Love is showing up for yourself when everything in you wants to give up. Love is holding your own hand through the storm. Love is being honest about your pain and giving yourself grace to heal.

I began to love myself in ways I never had before. Not just when I looked good or felt confident, but even in the moments I felt broken. I started journaling, meditating, going to therapy, surrounding myself with people who made me feel safe and seen. I built rituals around self-care—not the spa days or fancy things, but the quiet moments of checking in with my heart.

That self-love became my anchor. It gave me the strength to stop seeking validation from others and start standing firm in my truth. It allowed me to create boundaries, to say no, to walk away from things that didn't serve me — even if it hurt.

And that's when I discovered the true beauty of love: it starts within.

You cannot fully receive love from others until you learn how to give it to yourself. And you cannot expect others to hold your heart with care if you keep handing it to those who haven't even learned how to hold their own.

My losses didn't break me, they awakened me.

They taught me to be present. To cherish the little things. To love loudly and without apology. To stop hiding my scars and start wearing them like armor. Because every tear I cried, every moment I thought would destroy me, became a building block in my becoming. I also learned to lead with empathy. I can sit with someone in their sorrow and not rush to fix it, because I know the value of simply being seen. I know what it means to be held in a moment of pain, not with solutions, but with compassion.

These lessons weren't easy. They came with a price. But I wouldn't trade them. Because through it all, I found me. Not the version of me the world expected. Not the woman who always had to be strong or smile through the pain. But the real me — the one who is soft and strong, broken and whole, grieving and healing all at once.

To every woman who has loved deeply and lost quietly… who has smiled through heartbreak and kept showing up for life… who has felt like giving up but chose to keep breathing anyway — I see you.

You are not alone.

Your pain is valid. Your story matters. And your healing is possible.

You don't have to hide your scars to be strong.

You don't have to wear a mask to be worthy.

You are enough, exactly as you are — messy, complicated, healing, becoming.

And if you're still here — after all that tried to break you — then you still have work to do too.

Keep going. Your story isn't over. In fact, it's just beginning.

FOUR

COLLEGE, CAREER DREAMS & LOVE

Graduating from high school wasn't the finish line for me—it was just the warm-up. While many of her peers saw graduation as the end of their educational journey, I saw it as the launchpad. College wasn't optional. It was my way out and my way forward.

But getting there wasn't simple.

There were no silver spoons, trust funds, or family connections waiting for me. Just ambition, prayer, and a relentless determination to build a better life. So, when I packed up my dreams and headed for the University of North Texas, I brought all of my grit with me. I didn't know exactly how things would turn out—I just knew quitting wasn't one of my options.

UNT was a shift from the life I knew in Highland Hills. The campus was bigger, the people more diverse, and the possibilities wide open. For the first time, I was in an environment where dreaming big was normal—and that was refreshing. But that didn't mean the struggle disappeared.

College came with its own set of challenges: financial aid delays, long nights studying, and the silent stress of being a first-generation college student. I didn't have a blueprint. I had to figure it out on my own. From registering for classes to buying books, I was learning by trial and fire. And yet, I never wavered.

Her time at Navarro College was just as impactful. Juggling community college alongside her long-term goals taught her the value of flexibility and persistence. Whether I was on a big campus or a smaller one, I was always locked in. I wasn't just chasing a degree—I was chasing options, freedom, and financial peace.

I took a variety of classes, not yet knowing that one day I'd become a powerhouse in the financial space. But no matter what course I was enrolled in, one thing was clear: I was business minded. I had an eye for efficiency and a heart for service. The way professors talked about leadership, strategy, and systems—it sparked something in me. It wasn't just theory. It was destiny in disguise.

During my college years, I began to realize

something else: people were always coming to me for help. Whether it was classmates confused about FAFSA forms, friends needing help budgeting, or family asking questions about taxes, they all came to me. At first, it felt random. But over time, she began to see the pattern. She had a gift. A gift for breaking down what seemed complex and making it simple. A gift for financial clarity. My mom also has an accounting degree. She taught me some things as well. That spark started the fire. I then began to consider a career in finance or business. I didn't know exactly what shape it would take, but I knew I was meant to lead in a space that helped people grow, especially financially. And deep down, I started asking myself: Could this turn into a business? Could I really make money by helping others manage theirs?

The answer would soon reveal itself. But first, life had another lesson for her — love.
It was during this same season of becoming that I met someone who would change the course of her life: Byron Grant.

Byron wasn't just a love interest. He was a presence. A creative force in the music industry with ambition that matched her own. From the moment they met, I felt something different. He wasn't intimidated by my drive, he respected it. He saw my vision and didn't try to shrink it. He pushed me to be even greater.

Their connection was organic. They talked about everything, family, faith, hustle, pain, plans. They came from different worlds in some ways, but they both understood the pressure of chasing dreams while carrying real-life responsibilities. Byron's world of music was fast-paced and unpredictable, but he found grounding in my structure and wisdom. And I found comfort in his passion and creativity.

They were opposites in some ways but aligned where it mattered most.

As our relationship grew, I found myself balancing two types of building, building my future and building a relationship. And while some might have crumbled under the weight of both, I embraced it. Byron became more than a boyfriend. He became a partner in purpose. We talked about legacy, generational wealth, business plans, and family.

We didn't just fall in love. They grew into love — with intention.

I often reflect on how God's timing was at play. In the same season I discovered who I was professionally, I also had found someone who accepted and celebrated me fully. Byron wasn't trying to change me, he was clapping for me in every room that I walked into.

We eventually married, sealing not only our bond but our shared vision. It wasn't about a wedding—it was about a mission. Together, we would build something greater than themselves. Byron's music career would thrive. My business ideas would evolve. But at the center of it all was unity, support, and deep respect.

Even as love blossomed, I never lost sight of my grind. I eventually pursued and earned my Ph.D. in Lafayette, Louisiana, a milestone that symbolized more than education, represented endurance. All the late nights, all the early mornings, all the sacrifices all added up.

That degree didn't just hang on the wall. It spoke.

It said: You didn't fold.

It said: You chose the hard road.

It said: You did this for you, your family, and your future.

By the time I had my doctorate in my hand, I had already started planting the seeds for my business, Granted Tax Service. I knew that financial education and empowerment were missing in so many communities, especially in me. And I knew I was called to fill that gap.

But none of it — college, the degree, the marriage, the clarity — came easily.

It was the result of years of fighting for her future when it wasn't guaranteed. Of holding it together for others while building a foundation for myself. Of walking with faith when I didn't have a full plan, just a purpose. Looking back, I wouldn't trade those years for anything. Because they taught me how to balance love and leadership, academics and ambition, structure and spontaneity.

Most of all, they taught me this:

I don't have to choose between being smart, successful, and soft-hearted. You can be all of it. You can love deeply and still lead fiercely. I can pursue purpose and still make room for passion.

College wasn't just about books, it was about becoming.
And in that process, Dr. Burgundy Royster Grant was born.

FIVE

FROM TURBO TAX to TAX PRO

Sometimes, life doesn't announce your calling with a grand sign or a big moment. Sometimes, it starts with a random favor.

For Dr. Burgundy Royster Grant, it all began with a simple question:

"Hey, can you help me with my taxes?"

At the time, I didn't see myself as a tax expert. I was just someone who understood numbers, had a deep sense of responsibility, and had already been managing my own finances better than most adults twice my age. So, when a friend asked me to help with a TurboTax return, I said yes.

I sat down at the computer, entered the W-2 information, read through the questions, and clicked through the forms with the same analytical mindset I had applied to math and business classes. Before I knew it, the return was done. The refund came back quickly—and the friend was shocked. "Wait, that's how much I'm getting?"

I laughed, "I guess so!" What seemed like a casual favor turned into something much more. After that, word began to spread. "Yo, Burgundy did my taxes and got me right."

"She know what she is doing—she did it better than H&R Block."

"She charged way less and explained it better."

It wasn't long before people began coming to m not just with returns—but with questions. Real questions.

"What's the difference between a W-2 and 1099?"

"Why did I owe this year?"

"How can I get a bigger refund next time?"

At first, I felt unsure. "Am I even qualified to do this?" I asked myself. But the more I did, the more I realized: my skill wasn't just in data entry—it was in translation. I could take complicated tax language and make it make sense for everyday people. That was my superpower.

I began studying tax law more deeply. Not because anyone forced me to, but because I wanted to understand. I read IRS publications, watched YouTube tutorials, sat through webinars, and absorbed everything I could. This wasn't just a hobby anymore, it was a calling.

Still, the journey wasn't perfect. I made mistakes in the early years. Entered the wrong numbers. Missed credits. I even got a rejected return once because of a typo in a Social Security number. But each mistake became a lesson. And I didn't shy away from those hard moments—I embraced them.

"I'd rather mess up now and learn than pretend I know everything and stay stuck," I told myself.

I started keeping a notebook of every lesson

learned. Pages filled with tax codes, filing statuses, refund delays, and audit triggers. That notebook became my personal tax bible. And soon, it grew into the framework for what would eventually become my business.

What set me apart wasn't just my knowledge, it was my heart. I cared. When someone couldn't afford to pay me, I still helped. When a single mom was in tears because she owed money, she didn't understand, I sat with her for hours explaining every line of the return. I wasn't just doing taxes—I was serving people.

My apartment turned into a tax hub every

spring. Friends, family, and even strangers would drop by with envelopes of documents, receipts, pay stubs, and handwritten notes. I'd make coffee, put on gospel music, and work through returns like I was running my own office.

There was no storefront. No logo. No marketing plan. Just a girl with a laptop, a passion for numbers, and a deep desire to help my community navigate a system that wasn't built with them in mind.

By year three, I had processed over 100

returns—by myself.

I was now charging small fees. Still less than what big chains charged, but enough to show I knew my value. That money helped cover bills, gas, groceries, and more. But it wasn't about the cash—it was about the confirmation.

I began thinking:
What if I actually made this official?
What if I stopped treating this like a side hustle and treated it like a business?
What would it take to become a professional tax preparer?

That question led to certifications, continuing education, and a new level of confidence.

I enrolled in IRS-approved training, got her PTIN (Preparer Tax Identification Number), and studied the ethics and responsibilities that came with working on behalf of others. I wasn't playing games. I understood the risk of getting someone's taxes wrong — and I refused to operate with anything less than excellence.

Around this time, I started branding myself more intentionally. I created a name, began working on a website, and started preparing for something bigger.

That something would soon be called Granted Tax Service.
But before the name, the flyers, or the office space, there was just Burgundy and a laptop. My hands. My mind. My heart. And a neighborhood full of people who now trusted me more than they trusted major tax chains.

I also started to attract clients who were self-employed — hairstylists, barbers, artists, truck drivers. These weren't folks with clean-cut W-2s. They had 1099s, receipts in shoeboxes, side hustles, and cash app payments.

And that's when I discovered her niche.

I understood the entrepreneurs. I was one. And I knew that the tax world made them feel confused, left out, and often penalized for not having everything perfectly tracked.

So I created systems for them.

Simple worksheets.

Guides.

Budgeting tools.

I began to teach my clients — not just file for them. I showed them how to track expenses, why quarterly estimates mattered, how deductions worked, and how to protect themselves from audits.

I wasn't building a tax service — I was building a movement.

People left their appointments feeling empowered, not embarrassed. They came back the next year more prepared. Some even brought friends.

I realized something crucial: this wasn't just about taxes, it was about transformation.

And for the first time, I began to see the bigger

picture. I wasn't just preparing returns. I was preparing legacies.

By the time she filed her 300th return, I knew there was no turning back. I was no longer just "good with numbers."

I was a professional.

And soon, I'd be a CEO.

SIX

THE BIRTH of GRANTED TAX SERVICE

By the time I, Dr. Burgundy Royster Grant had helped hundreds of people file taxes, I knew it was time. What began as a favor, a side hustle, and a seat at a kitchen table had grown into something far more serious. The requests kept coming. The questions kept coming. The need kept growing.

And I wasn't just filling a gap — I was filling a void in the community.

It was time to stop playing small. I wasn't just "doing taxes." I was changing lives. And I needed a name that reflected both her authority and her assignment.

That's when Granted Tax Service was born.

The name had meaning. Deep meaning. "Granted" wasn't just her last name, it was symbolic.

It represented what her clients felt every time they left her office: permission. Permission to build wealth. Permission to learn. Permission to grow beyond fear, confusion, or lack.

Her clients didn't just leave with tax returns. They left with confidence, clarity, and a renewed sense of control.

Launching a business, though, came with real pressure. I wasn't some trust-fund entrepreneur or venture-capital-backed startup. I was self-funded, self-taught, and self-motivated. Every computer, every printer, every chair in her office was bought with her own money — or earned the hard way.

My first official location wasn't glamorous. It was functional. A modest space with just enough room for a desk, a waiting area, and a printer that needed constant encouragement. But to me, it was mines. It was more than an office—it was proof.

Proof that with discipline, a laptop, and a vision, a Black woman from Highland Hills could build something that mattered.

From day one, I have committed to three things:

1. *Education* – I wouldn't just prepare taxes; I would teach my clients what they were signing.

2. *Integrity* – I wouldn't lie, bend numbers, or chase fast refunds. I would build my business the right way.

3. *Excellence* – Every client—whether they made $12,000 or $120,000—would be treated like VIP.

It didn't take long for word to spread. Granted Tax Service became the place to go—not just during tax season but year-round. People came not just for refunds but for real financial guidance.

Single mothers. Retirees. Self-employed barbers and hairstylists. Nonprofit founders. Truck drivers. Teachers. Everybody came. And

I welcomed them all with professionalism, compassion, and the kind of wisdom that only comes from both experience and purpose.

She learned quickly that running a business meant wearing a hundred hats.

I was the tax preparer, the office manager, the marketing department, the janitor, the bookkeeper—and sometimes even the IT department. When the internet crashed, I fixed it. When a client was upset about a delay from the IRS, I calmed them down. When printers jammed, I rolled up her sleeves and got to work.

There were days I questioned it all.

Late nights when I couldn't sleep from the stress. Early mornings when I had to get up and smile, even when I was exhausted. I poured my own money into the business, sometimes working for free, just to build trust. And when the bank accounts got low, I relied on her faith and reminded myself why I started.

I didn't just want a business, I wanted a legacy.

I wanted my future children to see a mother who created something from nothing. I wanted my clients to stop living paycheck to paycheck.

I wanted my community to stop being afraid of the IRS and start taking control of their financial futures.

So I pushed. And I grew.

Soon, I was hiring staff — training them not just in tax law, but in how to care for people. I didn't want employees who just filled out forms. I wanted people who served. The office has grown. The client base grew. The impact grew.

And I stayed grounded. I still sat with clients

one-on-one. Still took late appointments for people working double shifts. Still answered panicked phone calls about audits. I was hands-on. Always.

My business didn't just survive, it thrived. I reinvested into branding, created systems, and began expanding my services — bookkeeping, business formation, tax strategy, and more. Granted Tax Service became more than just a tax office, it became a financial empowerment center.

And then the recognition started coming in. Local news articles. Online business rankings.

Community awards. Word-of-mouth testimonials that traveled across state lines. Burgundy Royster's name became synonymous with integrity and excellence in the tax industry.

But behind every win was a story. Behind every new client was a referral from someone who said, "She's the real deal." Behind every office upgrade was a sacrifice that most never saw.

Because I, Burgundy built my business the right way — from the ground up, brick by brick, client by client, truth by truth.

I didn't cut corners.

I didn't chase trends.

I focused on impact.

Even as the business scaled, my values stayed the same. Every tax season, I reminded my team:

"We don't just do taxes. We do transformation."

And that's what made Granted Tax Service different. It wasn't about how fast you got your refund. It was about how well you understood your future.

This chapter of Burgundy's journey wasn't just about building a brand. It was about owning my place at the table. About taking my seat in an industry that often overlooks women like me. About proving that a girl from Corsicana, raised in Highland Hills, could not only enter the financial world—but dominate it.

And yet, I knew this was only the beginning.

SEVEN

CLIMBING the BUSINESS LADDER

Starting a business is one thing. Scaling it is another. After successfully launching Granted Tax Service and building a solid reputation in my community, Dr. Burgundy Royster Grant stood at a crossroads. I had proven that I could run a tax business — now it was time to prove I could lead one.

The office was busy. The clients were loyal. The demand was rising. But I knew she couldn't do it alone forever. If I wanted to grow, I had to learn how to delegate, develop, and duplicate.

It was time to climb the business ladder.

The first major shift came with hiring. I had spent years doing everything myself — from data entry and appointments to marketing and customer service. But now, I needed a team. People I could trust. People who would treat my clients with the same respect, care, and professionalism I had poured into every single return.

The hiring process was intense. I didn't just want workers — I wanted ambassadors of her brand. Every resume, every interview, every hire was strategic. I trained them myself, often staying late to teach one-on-one sessions about IRS updates, client etiquette, and how to explain taxes in plain language.

My motto was clear –
"If you're on my team, you don't just represent Granted — you represent excellence."

Training new team members meant shifting my own mindset from doer to developer. That wasn't easy. Like many founders, I had to unlearn the belief that "no one can do it like I can." But growth requires trust. So, I trained, coached, corrected, and poured into my team until they were ready to take on more responsibility.

And they rose to the occasion.

Soon, I was no longer the only one preparing taxes. My team was stepping up, and my role began to evolve. I started focusing more on the business — systems, software, marketing, and expansion.

I built checklists, templates, and automations to streamline operations. I upgraded my client management systems. I adopted secure e-filing software to handle increased volume and protect sensitive data. I was no longer just a preparer—I was becoming a CEO.

But growth came with growing pains.

More clients meant more pressure. More staff meant more responsibility. There were late nights when I had to fix team mistakes. There were client complaints that hit hard. There were financial decisions that kept me up at night.

I was learning in real time how to balance leadership with longevity. Still, I didn't flinch.

I showed up every day. I kept leading team meetings, coaching my staff, and making sure the company's reputation stayed top tier. My clients didn't just come back—they brought their friends, their family, and even their business partners.

Granted Tax Service was no longer a small local shop—it was becoming a recognized brand.

With growth came vision. But I started thinking bigger. I expanded my services, adding credit restoration, business coaching, and financial literacy workshops. I hosted in-person and online training events. I spoke at community centers and business expos, teaching entrepreneurs how to structure their finances, protect their income, and plan for taxes year-round.

And then came a turning point: mentorship.

People began asking me to teach them how to do what I did. Aspiring tax professionals reached out from all over the country, wanting to know how to start their own tax businesses. At first, I shared tips here and there. But eventually, I realized: this is a whole new lane.

I began developing coaching programs — step-by-step guides to launching and growing a successful tax business. I shared the blueprints I had learned through trial, error, and prayer. I taught licensing, compliance, marketing, client management, and ethics. My coaching wasn't fluff — it was real, raw, and results-driven.

I didn't just create coaches — I created six-figure earners.

My name began to circulate in tax industry circles not just as a tax preparer, but as a tax coach and industry leader. I also mentored dozens — many of whom went on to launch their own offices, hire teams, and build financial independence for their families.

This new chapter of mentorship lit a fire in me. It combined everything that I loved — teaching, empowering, and creating impact on helping others scale. I then began to hold masterminds, host live Q&As and develop digital products that could reach hundreds at a time.

I became the coach I wished I had when I first started.

Even with the growth, I stayed rooted. I remained active in the day-to-day of Granted

Tax Service, still reviewing complex returns, still guiding clients through audits, and still stepping in when needed.

But now, I am also running the business with strategy and structure. I studied business operations, took leadership courses, and aligned myself with other successful entrepreneurs. I began to understand that to lead well, I had to grow personally and professionally.

I also started hiring not just for skill — but for culture. People who aligned with her values, her mission, and her no-nonsense approach to excellence. My team became more than staff — they became a family of financial professionals, united by purpose and powered by preparation.

With every hire, every system, and every season, Granted Tax Service moved from being just a tax office to a business ecosystem.

And Burgundy? I was no longer just climbing the ladder — I was building it for others.

EIGHT

CREATING "THE GRANT" METHODOLOGY

At a certain point in business, people don't just want your product, they want your process. As Dr. Burgundy Royster Grant continued scaling her business, coaching mentees, and helping thousands of clients, one question kept coming up:

"How do you do it?"

People weren't just asking how I filed taxes. They wanted to know how I structured my business, trained my team, built client trust, avoided burnout, and stayed true to my mission while still making money.

I realized I had a system — I had just never put it into words.

After sitting down, reflecting on years of trial, growth, and success, I found a pattern in everything I did. From client management to leadership, her approach followed a clear rhythm. That rhythm became a framework. And that framework became my signature formula:

The GRANT Methodology

Not just my last name — this acronym became a

blueprint for how to build, grow, and lead with purpose and profit in the tax and financial service industry.

Let's break it down:

G — Grounded in Integrity

Everything starts with trust.

From day one, I built my business with integrity. No shortcuts. No sketchy refunds. No chasing fast money at the expense of doing things right. I knew that in the tax world, integrity is currency.

Clients trusted me because I told them the truth—even when it wasn't what they wanted to hear. Employees respected me because I was led with transparency. My mentees followed me because they knew I wasn't just teaching the game—I was living it.

To be grounded in integrity meant I never compromised on values, even under pressure. It meant her business was built on ethics, not ego.

And that's what gave her longevity.

R — Results Over Hype

In the digital age, it's easy to sell a dream. But I believed in selling results.

I wasn't interested in flashy graphics or fake

flexing. I wanted my work to speak for itself. My clients didn't just get refunds, they got clarity. Her mentees didn't just get coaching, they got businesses. My team didn't just get jobs, they gained careers.

Every system, every product, every training I created was designed to work. No fluff. Just facts. The results became my reputation — and that reputation built an empire.

A — Accountability & Accuracy

I ran a tight ship — and for good reason. Taxes are not a game. One mistake can cost someone thousands, delay a refund, or trigger an audit. I trained my team, mentees, and clients to prioritize accuracy. I built systems to double-check work. I also created checklists, verification tools, and filing protocols.

But accuracy was only half the battle. The other half was accountability.

If something went wrong, I took ownership. And I expected the same from my staff. No blame games. No finger-pointing. Just solutions, growth, and responsibility.

That culture of accountability kept my business sharp and the team reliable.

N — Nurture the Client Relationship

I knew the difference between clients and

community.

Most tax professionals see people once a year. Not her. I built A year-round relationships. She followed up. I educated. I cared. My office wasn't just transactional, it was transformational.

From handwritten thank-you notes to personal check-ins during life events, I made my clients feel seen.

Even as the business scaled, I trained my team to remember birthdays, follow up on audits, and check in with returning clients. Because to me, clients weren't numbers — they were people.

And when people feel nurtured, they stay loyal.

T — Teach, Train, and Transform

At the core of my success was one truth: I was a teacher.

Whether I was walking a client through a Schedule C, training a new staff member, or coaching a mentee on how to open their first office, I always came with the heart of an educator.

The GRANT Methodology wasn't just a brand strategy—it was a ministry of knowledge.

I knew that teaching multiplies impact. It creates leaders, not followers. And transformation isn't just about money — it's about mindset.

Because once someone learns how to manage their finances, structure a business, or build generational wealth, they're never the same again.

Bringing the Method to Life

Once the GRANT Methodology was solidified, I began to weave it into everything I did.

- ☑ My staff training was centered on the GRANT pillars.
- ☑ My coaching programs taught tax professionals how to build businesses the GRANT way.
- ☑ My brand message became more consistent — clients knew exactly what to expect.

I created slide decks, course material, downloadable tools, and speaking topics around it. It became my differentiator in a saturated industry. Other tax professionals were offering transactions.

I was offering transformation.

And the results showed. My mentees started thriving. Clients raved about their experience. The staff became more confident and efficient. And other professionals in the industry began to take notice.

People weren't just asking, "Can you do my taxes?" They were asking, "Can you teach me the GRANT way?"

Why It Matters

For me, the GRANT Methodology wasn't just about branding. It was about honoring the journey.

It was a way to name the system that had carried me from a girl doing taxes on TurboTax to a nationally respected CEO, educator, and mentor.

It gave me business structure.

It gave me team direction.

It gave me students a path.

And most of all, it gave my legacy language.

Because long after the tax seasons pass and the refunds are spent, what will remain is this: A proven, principled way of doing business that serves people, builds wealth, and honors God.

That's the GRANT Method.

NINE

NATIONAL RECOGNITION & FEATURES

For years, Dr. Burgundy Royster Grant had worked in the shadows—not seeking applause, but impact. She had helped hundreds, then thousands, of clients with their taxes. Trained up a new generation of tax professionals. Built a thriving business from the ground up.

But eventually, excellence becomes too loud to ignore.

Recognition started slowly. A few kind words

on social media. Shout-outs from mentees. Clients telling others, "You need to go see Burgundy—she's different."

But then came something that changed everything: a call from KISH Magazine. They had been watching her work—her community impact, her leadership, her story. They wanted to feature her. Not just for her business, but for her resilience, faith, and powerful journey from struggle to success. When the article dropped, it felt surreal. There she was—Dr. Burgundy Royster Grant, on the pages of a respected publication, being honored for the very things she used to do quietly: serve, uplift, teach, and lead. The feature titled her as a "Trailblazer in Financial Empowerment." Her face, her story, her name—broadcast to thousands.

But Burgundy didn't let the spotlight blind her. She shared the article proudly, not as a brag, but as a beacon—a reminder to other women, especially Black women, that where you start doesn't determine where you can go.

She began receiving messages from readers across the country.

"Your story inspired me."

"I didn't know someone like me could make

it."

"Thank you for being visible. It gives me hope."

Burgundy realized that her story wasn't just hers anymore — it belonged to every underdog who had ever dared to dream.

And the features didn't stop there.

Soon, online business blogs, local news outlets, and Black-owned entrepreneur platforms began reaching out. Everyone wanted to know more about the woman who had gone from doing taxes at a kitchen table to building a respected brand with a national footprint.

Then came another moment that stopped her in her tracks: Granted Tax Service was ranked the Best Tax Preparation Business in Dallas, Texas, by Best Reviews.

It was more than a title. It was validation. Validation of every late night. Every training session. Every season she thought about giving up but didn't.

When she received the plaque, she thought of Highland Hills. She thought of her mother, Keon, working overtime to raise her. She thought of her younger siblings who now had proof that dreams really can turn into reality. And she thought of every client, team member, and mentee who believed in her.

That award wasn't just hers.

It belonged to the community she built.

Burgundy used that momentum to elevate everything. She rebranded her marketing, invested in digital campaigns, and positioned herself as more than just a tax preparer — she was now a thought leader in financial literacy and entrepreneurship.

She was invited to speak at panels, expos, women's conferences, and tax industry events.

Her calendar was filled with interviews, podcast features, and speaking engagements.

But no matter how far her name reached, she

remained grounded in the same principles that built her:

✅ Serve before selling

✅ Lead with purpose

✅ Never forget who you're doing it for

She would often tell her team, "It's not about being famous. It's about being faithful to the calling."

And that faithfulness opened more doors.

She became a trusted voice in the coaching world—especially for women starting financial businesses. Her coaching students began calling her "The Coach's Coach." Some were earning six figures within their first two seasons. Others were finally leaving 9-to-5 jobs, opening storefronts, and changing their families' financial trajectories.

Burgundy's recognition became a reflection of her ripple effect.

But with recognition came new challenges. The more visible she became, the more pressure she felt to maintain excellence. People had expectations. Clients wanted access. Mentors wanted partnerships. The community looked to her for answers.

She leaned on God even more in this season. She stayed prayed up, stayed covered, and made sure she had the right voices around her. Byron, her husband, became her grounding force—reminding her to rest, to stay focused, and to protect her peace.

She also protected her standards. No matter how public her name became, she never lowered the bar. Her business remained compliant. Her team stayed trained. Her message stayed real.

Because Burgundy knew you can be celebrated one day and canceled the next if your foundation isn't solid.

So she continued building her brand with integrity. She didn't chase clout. She let her work speak. And her work continued to echo — across cities, states, and industries.

At one speaking event, a woman approached her in tears.

"You have no idea what it means to see a woman who looks like me, sounds like me, and made it. You didn't just give me advice — you gave me permission."

That moment reminded Burgundy why she shared her story publicly in the first place. Visibility wasn't about ego — it was about representation.

And in every magazine article, every award, every keynote, Burgundy carried a simple mission:

Show what's possible.

Not perfection.

Possibility.

For the single mom just trying to make ends meet.

For the college student hustling between classes and side gigs.

For the hairstylist with a shoebox of receipts and no idea how to file.

For the woman in the hood with a laptop and a vision.

Burgundy Royster Grant had become more than a name—she was a movement.

And the world had taken notice.

TEN

BECOMING A COACH, A CEO and AN AUTHOR

What started as a favor on TurboTax evolved into something much greater. For Dr. Burgundy Royster Grant, this journey was never just about taxes. It was about transformation—hers and everyone else's she encountered along the way.

From the early days of preparing returns in her home to becoming one of the most trusted names in the tax industry, Burgundy's story is not only one of business growth, but of personal evolution.

She was no longer just a tax preparer.

She was no longer just a business owner.

She had stepped fully into her role as a Coach, a CEO, and now, an Author.

The Coach

Coaching came naturally to Burgundy. Long before she labeled herself a mentor, people were already learning from her — watching how she worked, listening to her advice, and modeling their businesses after hers.

But it wasn't until she formally launched her

coaching programs that the full power of her influence became clear.

Her coaching was different. It wasn't rooted in hype, gimmicks, or surface-level "motivation." It was real. She taught tax professionals how to set up legal structures, comply with IRS requirements, market with integrity, and deliver results clients would come back for year after year.

She didn't just give information—she gave her mentees confidence.

She showed them how to go from taking

clients at their kitchen table to owning full-fledged offices.

From undercharging and overwhelmed to six figures and self-assured.

Her students were growing faster than they imagined — earning more, expanding quicker, and most importantly, building businesses that actually lasted.

They weren't just learning tax law — they were learning the GRANT Methodology, the system that had carried Burgundy from survival to scale.

And the testimonials poured in:

"Because of Dr. Burgundy, I finally understand taxes."

"She believed in me before I believed in myself."

"I quit my job and went full-time because of her coaching."

This was more than a business program—it was a calling.

Burgundy became a safe space, a sounding board, and a strategist. She was "the coach's coach." The one who didn't just teach you how to get clients—but how to keep them, how to grow, and how to lead with purpose.

The CEO

As her influence grew, so did her business. Running a company on a scale requires a new level of thinking. Burgundy was no longer the only person preparing taxes — she was overseeing teams, managers, departments, and digital systems.

She invested in better technology. Upgraded her client portals. Created SOPs (standard operating procedures). Every department at Granted Tax Service was being shaped by her leadership.

Her team expanded — from part-time seasonal

help to full-time, year-round staff. And each member was trained not just in tax prep—but in culture. Burgundy's core values—integrity, accuracy, and education—were the foundation of every client's interaction.

As CEO, she learned how to lead leaders. How to make high-level decisions. How to delegate without losing personal touch. And how to maintain profitability without compromising people.

She embraced strategy calls, financial forecasting, and brand licensing. She understood marketing funnels, email automations, course platforms, and digital sales. Her business mind sharpened with every move.

And she made sure to bring her team with her. Whether it was an intern or a senior staff member, everyone around Burgundy learned how to lead by watching her do it first. She modeled composure under pressure, discernment in decisions, and compassion with clients.

She was building more than a business — she was building a movement powered by leadership.

The Author

There comes a time in every leader's journey when the message becomes too big to hold inside.

For Burgundy, authoring a book wasn't about adding a title to her name — it was about documenting the blueprint. It was about putting her story in the hands of people who needed hope, guidance, or a path forward.

She knew there were young women out there like her — born in places the world overlooks, raised by mothers who did their best, and carrying dreams that felt too heavy at times.

She knew there were tax professionals who were brilliant but stuck, ethical but underpaid, and ready for more but unsure how to reach it.

She knew there were entrepreneurs looking for structure, for mentorship, for someone who had actually done it — and done it the right way.

So she began to write.

This very book you're reading is the culmination of everything she's lived, learned, and led.

From Corsicana to Highland Hills…

From kitchen-table tax returns to national

recognition…

From being the oldest sibling to being the family foundation…

From helping one person on TurboTax to building a coaching empire…

This is her story.

This is her system.

This is her legacy in ink.

A Legacy Beyond Numbers

Burgundy's story proves that success isn't reserved for the privileged.

It's reserved for the prepared, the resilient, the faithful, and the focused.

She didn't get here by accident. She worked.

She studied. She cried. She sacrificed. She showed up when it was hard. She served when it wasn't easy. She led when no one clapped.

And now, she stands as a CEO, a mentor, a coach, a wife, a woman of God, and now an author—not just building a brand, but building a legacy that lives on.

Her message to you, the reader?
"Start where you are. Use what you have. Honor who you are. And lead with what you know.

You don't need permission. You've already been granted."

ELEVEN

BORN for A PURPOSE

They told my mama I might not make it through the night.

I wasn't supposed to be here.

My original due date was February 12, 1992, but I showed up on December 9, 1991 — tiny, fragile, two months too early. Barely big enough to hold. Barely strong enough to breathe. The doctors watched me closely, whispering things my mama wasn't supposed to hear. Words like "critical" and "uncertain." But God had other plans.

That first night was supposed to be my last. But the sun rose, and so did I. I was fighting before I even knew what life was. My mama, Kian, sat by my incubator, praying, promising, whispering my name. She didn't have much, but she gave me the only thing that mattered love and the will to keep going.

That was my first lesson –

I was born a fighter.

By the time I was two years old, the world had already tried to take me again.

My mama was working, trying to keep a roof over our heads. She left me with my aunt for the day. But toddlers are curious, and curiosity has no fear.

I got out of the apartment. Just wandered off.

And there it was: a swimming pool. Six feet deep. Shimmering blue. Silent and still. I couldn't swim. I didn't think about that.

I was two years old — what did I know about danger?

I leaned over. Then I jumped.

Cold water wrapped around me. It filled my ears, my nose, my lungs. I sank.

They say drowning is quiet. They're right.

There's no dramatic splashing. Just silence and sinking.

I remember the weight. I remember the blur of light above me. I remember thinking — this is it.

But God sent a stranger.

A man and his family were there, by chance — or maybe not by chance at all. He saw me. He jumped in. He pulled me out.

I drowned. But I didn't die.

He breathed life back into me. My tiny chest rose again. Water poured out of me. And I lived.

Looking back now, those two moments — the night I was born and the day I drowned, bookends to the story of my life. They're proof that I wasn't supposed to be here… but I am. It's not a coincidence. It's not luck. It's purpose.

God marked me before I even knew His name. He was telling me:

"Daughter, you're going to walk through fire." You're going to be attacked. You're going to be broken. But you're also going to rise. Because I've given you a purpose."

As I grew older, I didn't always understand why life felt so hard. Why were the odds always stacked against me. Why I had to fight so much, so young.

But when I trace my story back, I see it clearly now. Those early moments were training. They were seeds. They were the first signs that my life would not be ordinary.

You don't survive premature birth by accident. You don't survive drowning at two years old by chance. You survive because there is more for you to do.

That realization has guided me ever since. When things got hard in Highland Hills, I remembered: I'm supposed to be here.

When I sat in classrooms where teachers doubted me, I remembered: I'm supposed to be here.

When I built a business from nothing, when I faced setbacks, when I felt alone, I remembered: I'm still here.

And if I'm still here, there's a reason.

Every milestone I've achieved — every degree, every business, every person I've coached — is rooted in that truth.

My survival isn't just survival. It's testimony.

And that testimony fuels my purpose.

People sometimes ask me, "Where do you get your drive from? How do you keep going?"

I smile and say, "I've been fighting since birth."

Because it's true.

My story began with two near-deaths and a God who wouldn't let me go. It began with a mother's prayers and a stranger's rescue. It began with tiny lungs learning to breathe and a toddler pulled from a pool.

Everything after that—every setback, every betrayal, every victory—has been built on that foundation.

Now, when I stand on stages, when I mentor women, when I lead my team, I'm not just teaching tax preparation or business strategy. I'm teaching survival. I'm teaching resilience. I'm teaching purpose.

I'm showing that where you start doesn't define where you finish—and what tries to kill you can become the thing that fuels you.

I shouldn't be here.

But I am.

And because I am, I will use this life for more than just myself. I will use it to serve, to teach, to empower, to leave a legacy.

Because purpose is never just about you.

It's about everyone who tells you your story will touch.

And if you're reading this, maybe it's touching you right now.

I want you to know something:

If you've survived something that should've killed you — physically, emotionally, spiritually — you are not an accident.

You're evidence.

Evidence of a plan bigger than the pain.

Evidence that you're not done yet. Evidence that you're still here for a reason.

So I keep going. For the little girl in the incubator. For the toddler at the bottom of the pool. For the teenager staring at the wall. For the woman authoring this book.

I keep going because every breath is borrowed grace. And I refuse to waste it. That's my truth. That's my beginning. That's my purpose.

TWLEVE

BROKEN but STILL STANDING

I built a life with him. I chose him. I believed in him. But nothing prepared me for the moment I found out the man I loved — the man I married — had cheated on me and fathered a child outside our home.

Nothing.

There's a type of heartbreak that doesn't just sting. It rips. It cracks you in half, splinters your sense of trust, and leaves your soul scattered on the floor like broken glass. That was me.

I wasn't hurt. I was humiliated. I was enraged. I was wrecked. And yet, somehow, I still had to get up the next day… and be Dr. Burgundy Royster Grant.

The Moment Everything Shifted

I can't tell you exactly what day it was, because honestly, it's a blur now. What I remember is the weight. That thick, silent tension in the air before the truth is spoken. The cold sweat of intuition.

And then the confirmation: He cheated. There was another woman. And there was a child. Not a rumor. Not a maybe. A baby. A living, breathing symbol of betrayal.

I felt like I was suffocating. Like someone had taken a sledgehammer to my chest and then expected me to breathe through the pain.

I was angry. I was broken. And I was alone with it.

Because when you're a wife, a CEO, a coach, a leader, a visionary — there's no "day off" for grief. There's no collapse button.

People still expect you to show up. And I did.

But it took everything.

Grieving While Leading

I remember hosting a training course the same week I found out.

My eyes were swollen. My heart was bleeding.

But my clients didn't know. My staff didn't know. The world didn't know.

I smiled through it. I coached through it. I survived through it.

And every time I closed my laptop or left the office, I would collapse on my bed and just sob.

Grief doesn't care about your calendar.

Betrayal doesn't wait until after tax season.

The War Inside Me

There were moments I wanted to throw it all away. Not just the marriage — everything. My business. My brand. My platform.

Because how could I keep preaching about empowerment when I felt so powerless in my own home?

How could I coach women on building legacy when mine was falling apart?

But then I remembered: I'm not just building this for me. I'm building it from everything I've survived.

And this? This was just another war.

And I've always been a warrior.

The Choice to Stay

People will judge me for staying. Some already have.

They'll say I'm weak. They'll say I'm settling.

But what they don't know is what I know.

They don't know the nights we prayed together. The apologies I watched him choke on. The work he did — not just words, but work.

Forgiveness isn't a one-time thing. It's daily. It's layered. And it's exhausting. But I chose to stay.

Not because I forgot. Not because I'm naive.

But because I saw the man behind the mistake, and because I know what kind of woman I am. And I accepted that child—not as a shame, not as a symbol of pain, but as a life. She didn't ask to be here. She didn't cause the damage. And I will not punish her for the mistake of adults.

I chose to love her. To accept her as my own. To be a woman of grace in a moment that could've hardened me completely.

I'm Not the Same Woman

Something died in me that day. But something else was born.

A woman who knows her worth so deeply, she doesn't need public approval. A woman who can love deeply and still set boundaries. A woman who can be broken and still build empires.

I lost something in that moment — but I gained clarity. I gained a new version of myself. A tougher, wiser, more spiritually grounded version.

And though the pain still shows up in waves, I now ride them instead of drowning in them.

To Every Woman Reading This…

If you've ever been betrayed, I see you. If you've ever screamed in silence because your image couldn't handle your pain, I know that scream. If you've ever had to wipe your tears and host a meeting right after, I stand with you.

You're not weak. You're not crazy. You're not alone.

You are simply a woman who loved. And love, when betrayed, cuts the deepest. But don't you ever let that pain convince you that you're not powerful. Because you still are.

Business Still Had to Run

Even while I was hurting, the business couldn't pause.

Clients still had questions. Software still had glitches. My team still needed leadership.

So I put on the lashes. I showed up to the office. I shot the promo videos. I encouraged my mentees.

I did it while bleeding.

Some days, I'd go to the bathroom in between meetings just to cry.

Then I'd come back, fix my face, and get back to work. Because that's what leaders do. That's what I do.

I didn't fake my strength. I just had to live in it.

Private Pain, Public Strength

Social media will have you thinking success is always polished.

But behind every "Boss Babe" post is a woman who's battled storms no one ever sees. Behind every branded logo is a woman who wanted to give up—but didn't.

Behind me—is a woman who had to forgive someone she trusted, and then find the strength to keep loving herself in the process.

It's not easy. It's not cute. But it's real.

And this is why I tell my story. Because somebody else out there is crying in silence. And I want you to know: you're not the only one.

What I've Learned

1. Healing is not linear. Some days you'll feel okay. Other days, you'll remember everything and break again. That's normal. That's human.

2. Staying is a decision, not a weakness. Forgiveness isn't forgetting. It's deciding what your future deserves more than what your past demands.

3. Your purpose can still thrive in pain. I didn't lose clients. I didn't lose my vision. If anything, I became more powerful because I led through the fire.

4. Your heart is still yours. You don't have to let betrayal define you. You can still love, still grow, still believe.

To My Husband

You broke me. But you also stood with me while I put myself back together.

You looked me in the eyes and took full accountability. You didn't run. You didn't deflect. You faced the storm you created — and I saw your regret.

I saw your willingness to rebuild. And I made the choice to let you. We're still together. And it hasn't been easy. But we're doing the work.

That doesn't erase the past. But it gives hope to the future.

And I'm proud of both of us — for fighting for what most people would've walked away from.

Still Standing

If you've ever looked at me and thought I was unbreakable, let me be honest: I broke. But I healed. And now I'm standing taller.

Not because I'm perfect. But because I refused to let pain make me bitter. I let it make me better.

Final Words

This chapter of my life wasn't on the vision board. It wasn't part of the six-figure plan. But it happened. And it shaped me.

So I'm writing it down—not as a wound, but as a witness. Because somebody needs to know you can survive the things you thought would kill you.

You can build your dream while mending your heart. You can lead while you heal. You can cry and still conquer.

I'm proof of that.

I'm still standing.

THIRTEEN

THE DAY EVERYTHING CHANGED

I was born into hustle. Not just survival — but strategy.

My mom wasn't just any woman from the hood. She was a boss. A street queen. A real-life hustler who moved with the kind of precision that made men follow her lead and fear her power.

While most girls were playing dolls and braiding hair, I was learning how to count money, how to watch hands, and how to move in silence. My mama didn't raise a dummy.

She raised me in a world of sharp instincts, fast decisions, and unspoken codes.

She was a drug dealer. But to me, she was the hardest working woman I had ever known.

She made sure I had what I needed. She handled her business. And she did it all while looking fly and keeping her head high.

But I'll never forget the day the Feds came. Because that was the day my childhood ended.

My 13th Birthday

It was supposed to be a day of celebration. I had just turned thirteen. I was a teenager now. But before I could even enjoy the morning, everything came crashing down. BOOM. BOOM. BOOM.

The loud bangs on our front door didn't sound like knocking. They sounded like war.

I knew something was wrong instantly. The house shook. Windows rattled. My stomach dropped.

The Feds didn't come to talk. They came to take.

And they came for my mama.

The Raid

It was chaos. Guns drawn. Voices screaming.

The air was thick with tension and fear.

I stood frozen as they busted down the front

door. Everything after that felt like a blur and a

movie all at once.

My mama — always ten steps ahead — had tried

to hide under our house.

We had a trap door under the hallway rug.

Most people didn't know it existed. But we

used to crawl under there to stash things or

hide when the streets got too hot.

I watched as she lifted that rug and

disappeared under the house, like a shadow

slipping out of sight.

But the Feds weren't playing that day. They knew. They were ready.

I stood by the couch watching them pull her out—by her legs. They yanked her like she wasn't even human.

They tossed her onto the bed. Slapped handcuffs on her wrists. Didn't even let her fix her shirt.

And in that moment, I saw something I had never seen before.

My mama—my hero, my teacher, my protector—was no longer in control. She was helpless.

And suddenly, so was I.

The Silence After

After they left, everything was quiet.

No more yelling. No more footsteps. Just me.

Alone. At 13. On my birthday. And the silence screamed louder than anything else ever had.

There was no birthday cake. No candles. No singing.

Just a half-open trap door, a broken lock, and a teenage girl sitting on the couch trying not to fall apart.

That's when I knew — I wasn't a little girl anymore.

I had to grow up. Fast.

Becoming the Woman of the House

With my mom gone, there was no plan. No backup guardian. No family lineup to come save the day.

It was just me.

I learned quickly how to survive. I figured out how to keep the lights on — for a while. I ate whatever I could find. I kept the house clean in case someone came by.

But the truth is, I was a child trying to hold up a collapsing world.

And every night, I'd lay in that house, thinking about what had just happened, thinking about where my mama was, and wondering if she was okay, if she missed me if she was coming back.

The streets had swallowed her up. And all I had were my memories.

What My Mama Taught Me

Despite everything, I loved her deeply.

Because even though she was out there hustling, she always came home to me. She showed me loyalty. She showed me independence. She showed me how to handle business.

I know now that she did what she thought she had to do.

Life didn't hand her a silver spoon. It handed her survival — and she turned it into power.

She taught me how to count money. How to read people. How to move smart.

And even though that world took her away from me, it also gave me some of the grit I still carry today.

The Decision I Made That Day

As I sat on the couch that night, I remember whispering to myself – "I'm going to be different."

Not because I hated where I came from. But because I knew I had to build something better.

I had to break cycles. I had to break patterns. I had to break free.

That night, I didn't know I'd one day become a CEO. I didn't know I'd mentor hundreds of women. I didn't know I would author a book about it.

All I knew was that I had pain, and a choice.

And I chose to use my pain as fuel.

The Girl Who Survived the Knock

Every time I think about my 13th birthday, I feel two things: 1. Sadness—for what was stolen. 2. Pride—for the woman I became.

That knock on the door wasn't just the Feds. It was destiny. It was pain wrapped in purpose. That moment marked the beginning of my fire. The kind of fire that can't be bought, can't be broken, and can't be faked.

It's why I grind the way I do. It's why I don't play when it comes to legacy. It's why I pour into others because I know what it feels like to be empty.

I was 13 years old. And my world got flipped upside down.

But I made it.

I'm still making it.

And I'll never stop.

Final Words

This chapter of my life is not fiction. It's not entertainment. It's truth.

It's a piece of my soul I'm handing to the world. So that some young girl, sitting in silence, knows she's not alone.

If your foundation gets snatched away, you can still rise. If you lose your first protector, you can still become your own hero. If the streets break you, you can still rebuild from the rubble.

I'm living proof. And I'm not done yet.

FOURTEEN

CHRISTMAS LOST ITS MAGIC

The lights, the cold air, the joy in the streets—even in our hood, you could feel the holiday spirit trying to dance through the chaos.
But Christmas morning when I was thirteen years old, that's the day magic died for me. That's the morning I learned that silence can be deafening, that love can betray you, and that sometimes the monsters don't live under your bed—they sleep beside you.

My mom, **Kian**, was gone.

She had gotten caught up in the streets, chasing survival, making decisions she never wanted to explain and I never wanted to ask about. She was arrested. Just like that — *vanished*.

And I was left in that house, **alone**.

Alone for **six weeks**.

The lights got cut off. The water stopped running. The food was gone. But I stayed. I figured out how to bathe with bottles of water, how to study by candlelight, how to keep people from finding out I was living like this.

I told no one. I was scared that if I said

something, the system would take me away.

I was thirteen.

Trying to be grown.

Trying to survive.

I kept telling myself: *He's going to come get me.*

My daddy.

Any day now.

But day after day, week after week, he didn't.

Not until everything had shut down.

Not until there was nothing left to lose.

Not until I started to think maybe I didn't

matter anymore.

That's when he showed up.

No hugs. No apology. No "I'm sorry you've been living like this."

Just, "Come on."

I packed what little I had, and we left. I was numb. Just... numb.

That night, **Christmas Eve**, we stayed at his house.

There was only one room for me to sleep in.

And in that room — one bed.

I didn't think much of it. He was my dad. Even though I didn't really *know* him like a daughter should. Even though he never showed up like a real father should. He was still my blood. He was all I had at that moment.

I lay in that bed. Fully clothed. Facing the wall.

And then it happened.

5:00 a.m.

I still remember the exact time. I had cracked one eye open and glanced at the red numbers glowing from the digital clock.

He thought I was asleep.

I felt him shift behind me. The bed creaked.

Then—

His hand.

Moving slowly.

I felt it on my butt.

Not accidental. Not fatherly.

Intentional.

He was testing me.

Would I move?

Would I say something?

I didn't. I froze.

My body turned concrete, but my mind was screaming.

No. No. No.

This isn't happening.

He wouldn't… He can't…

But he did.

He touched me. My father. The man who was supposed to protect me. The man who didn't come for me when the lights went out. The man who left me alone, then touched me when he finally showed up.

I stared at the wall. Eyes wide open. Paralyzed by betrayal. I wanted to run. I wanted to disappear. But I just... lay there. Frozen in shock.

That morning became a scar I would carry for the rest of my life.

I said nothing.

Not that day. Not the next.

I kept it all inside.

Because what would happen if I told?

Would anyone believe me?

Would they say I was fast? A liar?

Would I be taken away from the little bit of stability I had left?

So I locked it away.

But trauma doesn't stay buried. It leaks.

It leaked into how I trusted people.

Into how I overachieved in school.

Into how I smiled too hard to cover what I was afraid to say out loud.

I kept showing up. Strong. Smart. Capable.

But behind my eyes, I was still that little girl staring at the wall, silently screaming in the dark.

Years passed. And still, I didn't tell.

But the memory told on me.

In the way I pulled away when people hugged me too tight.

In the way I slept with lights on for years.

In the way I poured myself into other people's problems—because I didn't know how to fix my own.

I became successful. Driven. Focused.

But deep down, I was still carrying a little girl who had never gotten to heal.

And then one day—I broke.

Not loud. Not in front of a crowd.

But quietly.

In my car.

Alone.

I sobbed so hard I couldn't breathe. I beat the steering wheel with my fists.

I screamed from the place where the silence had lived too long.

And then, I made a choice:

I was going to stop hiding her.

I was going to stop protecting the man who hurt me.

I was going to **own my voice**.

That's why this chapter is here.

Not for shock.

Not for sympathy.

But for **freedom**.

For the 13-year-old me.

And for every woman or man who was violated and told to be quiet.

For everyone who heard "that didn't happen" or "get over it."

For every survivor who never got a chance to scream.

This is for us.

Healing didn't come all at once.

It came in therapy. In prayer. In surrender.

It came in forgiving *myself* for thinking it was my fault.

It came in forgiving *my mother* — because as much as it hurt, I know she was fighting her own demons.

It came when I looked in the mirror and said:

"You were a child.

You deserved protection.

What happened was not your fault."

I started writing.

Speaking.

Coaching.

Leading.

I became the woman I needed when I was that little girl.

And now?

I'm not ashamed.

Because this pain no longer controls me.

So, to the girl who's still silent:

You are not dirty.

You are not weak.

You are not alone.

To the woman who never told her story:

You don't owe the world your pain, but you *do* owe yourself your healing.

To the mother who carries guilt:

You are still worthy of redemption.

To the child in all of us who froze in the dark:

You survived.

And survival is sacred.

I am Dr. Burgundy Royster Grant.

I am a businesswoman. A wife. A coach. A CEO.

I help people build legacies.

I help people file taxes.

But more than anything — **I help people find power in their truth**.

This chapter is mine. And now, I give you permission to write yours.

Because you've been silent long enough.

ABOUT THE AUTHOR

Dr. Burgundy Royster is a nationally recognized tax strategist, entrepreneur, and educator. She is the Founder and CEO of Granted Tax Service, a firm known for its integrity-driven approach to tax preparation, strategy, and financial empowerment. With years of experience serving individuals, entrepreneurs, and small business owners, Dr. Royster has built a reputation for translating complex tax concepts into clear, actionable guidance.

Beyond client services, Dr. Royster is a sought-after coach and mentor to tax professionals nationwide. She trains and equips emerging preparers and firm owners to build compliant, scalable, and purpose-driven businesses through education, systems, and leadership development. Her work emphasizes accuracy, accountability, and long-term sustainability in an industry often driven by short-term results.

As a business leader, Dr. Royster is committed to helping others move from survival to structure, and from income to legacy. Her professional mission is rooted in empowerment—ensuring that knowledge, discipline, and strategy are accessible tools for growth. *You've Been Granted* represents the intersection of her lived experience and the professional principles that guide her work.

For speaking engagements, training, or event bookings, contact:
burgundy@grantedtaxservice.com

www.ingramcontent.com/pod-product-compliance
Lightning Source LLC
Chambersburg PA
CBHW072044160426
43197CB00014B/2622